MW00574976

A First Book of
SCHUMANN

32 Arrangements for the Beginning Pianist

DAVID DUTKANICZ

DOVER PUBLICATIONS, INC.
Mineola, New York

To Maria

Copyright

Copyright © 2010 by Dover Publications, Inc.
All rights reserved.

Bibliographical Note

A First Book of Schumann: 32 Arrangements for the Beginning Pianist is a
new work, first published by Dover Publications, Inc., in 2010.

International Standard Book Number

ISBN-13: 978-0-486-47905-7
ISBN-10: 0-486-47905-6

Manufactured in the United States by Courier Corporation
47905601
www.doverpublications.com

Contents

Works are arranged in order of approximate difficulty

Editor's Note

The music of Robert Schumann (1810–1856) holds a special place in piano literature. Prior to 1840, his published compositions were exclusively for solo piano. Within these are numerous works that have become cornerstones of the instrument's pedagogy, most notably *Scenes from Childhood*, *Album for the Young*, and *Carnaval*. Schumann never wrote a method or book of exercises, opting to develop technique through melodically meaningful music. As a father (and piano teacher) of eight, he had a keen insight into the needs of beginners.

As part of Dover's renowned series, this edition is meant to make Schumann's canon accessible and enjoyable to a greater audience. These carefully selected and arranged pieces are designed to develop both fingers and ears, keeping in spirit with the composer. Most focus on a particular skill: e.g., odd time signatures in *Eusubius*, dynamics in *Horseman,* and composite rhythms in *Chiarina.* Fingerings are provided as suggestions, although each individual will discover what works best. Phrasing and pedaling have also been left open so as to make the music less daunting. These can be filled in as each piece progresses.

From a Foreign Land

This is the first of 13 childhood reminisces composed by Schumann. They were called *Scenes from Childhood* ("Kinderszenen"). He had eight children of his own, and wrote many pieces for them *and* about them.

Moderato

Important Events

Andante means "at a walking pace." Notice how the melody "walks" from a high G down to a middle G. Pay attention to the sharps that turn the directions of this stroll.

Child Falling Asleep

With so many children, Clara and Robert Schumann had much practice putting them to bed. Schumann creates a lulling effect with a repeated passage in the right hand known as an *ostinato*. This piece ends on a peaceful, eye-shutting major chord.

Slowly and Gently

Traumerei

The title means "dream" and it is the best-known work from this collection. Play it in a sweet and "dreamy" manner, without rushing. Keep the melody light, and swell the dynamics.

Calmly

The Poet Speaks

This is the finale of *Scenes from Childhood.* Schumann as a grown-up poet, is saying goodbye to his childhood. Before playing, look over the "grown-up" accidentals in the music.

Lonely Flowers

The forest has always been a magical place where many fairy tales have been set. Schumann was inspired by the woods, and wrote a collection of pieces called *Forest Scenes*. Picture a storybook background when playing the swaying melody.

Slow and expressive

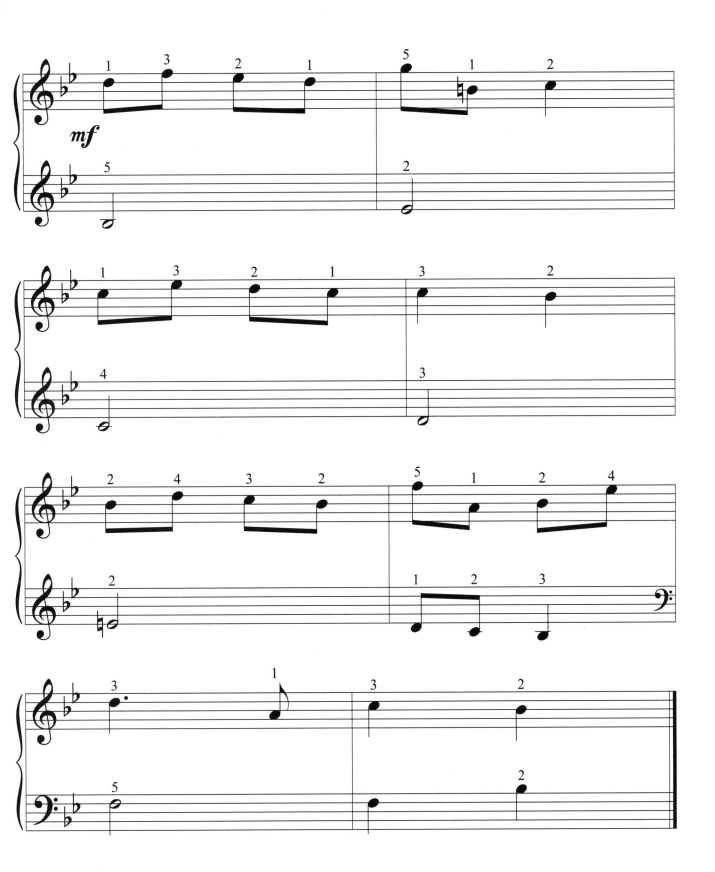

Hunting Song

In the past, the hunt was announced with a bugle call. This would gather the hunters at the edge of the forest and alert others for safety. Play the melody brightly, just like a bugle or trumpet.

Vivace

Children's Sonata

Schumann wrote a short sonata for three of his daughters. He would give them piano lessons and compose pieces tailored to each. This one was dedicated to Julie.

Allegro moderato

Kreisleriana No. 8

This sprightly piece is based on a fictional musician named Johannes Kreisler. He was a character created by novelist E.T.A. Hoffman—the author of the *Nutcracker* story. Schumann himself was an aspiring writer before he became a composer.

Allegro

Eusubius

This may be the first time you've seen a $\frac{7}{4}$ time signature, but don't be nervous. It's simply a melody that is three beats plus four. Follow the dashed lines when counting and you'll be able to subdivide the measures easily.

Adagio

Chopin

The composer Chopin was a friend of Schumann's, and this piece was written in his style to honor him. Interpret the section marked "freely" in any speed you like. Just return back to the original at "a tempo."

Allegro

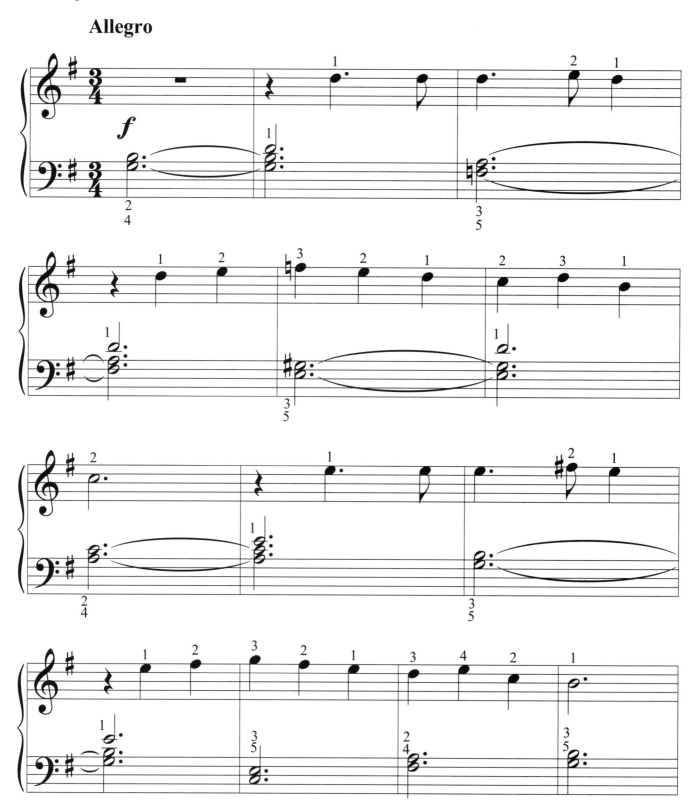

Chiarina

Schumann wrote this charming work for his future wife, who just happened to be his piano teacher's daughter. Follow the angled lines to keep track of the pulse as it moves from right hand to left. Hint: first play the right hand without ties to feel the proper rhythm.

With feeling

Valse Allemande

The title of this lively piece means "German Waltz." Dances in this style were played at parties and masquerades where everyone joined in. Keep the tempo lively and toe-tapping.

Lively and light

Marche Davide

Schumann created a half-imaginary musical society known as the "League of David." Most of the works in *Carnaval* are portraits of its members. This piece was dedicated to them, as they marched off to battle their own half-imaginary Goliaths.

Stately

Stately

Der Arme Peter

The title of this piece means "Poor Peter" and is the setting of a Heinrich Heine poem. It tells the sad story of a boy walking through a village, disappointed over his lost love. Keep the mood pastoral and melancholic.

Jemand

from Myrthen

This is a song Schumann dedicated to his wife from a collection called *Myrthen*—evergreens whose branches flowered and were used as wedding wreaths. *Jemand* means "someone special." Play these special images warmly.

Melodie

This charming work is the first of 43 melodic lessons Schumann wrote for his daughters: Marie, Elise, and Julie. At first, even these weren't easy for them. Remember to have patience, and you'll see how quickly you improve.

Moderato

Little Piece

When playing, take advantage of rests as a chance to look ahead and reposition your hands—but don't forget to keep counting! The left hand might feel bumpy, but keep your wrists moving smoothly and the right hand lyrical.

Horseman

Dynamics are always key to musical interpretation. This work recreates the sound of a passing horseman by getting louder during the approach and softer for the departure. The heavy and light sections emphasize this image.

Short and brisk

The Poor Orphan

This piece is written in a minor key, which, unlike major keys, usually sounds sad. Be expressive, and listen to the mood that Schumann is creating. The title should help.

Chorale

Chorales are pieces written for four voices. From the top down they are: Soprano, Alto, Tenor and Bass. When two stems are on one note, it means both voices are singing the same note. This is known as *unison*.

Slowly and stately

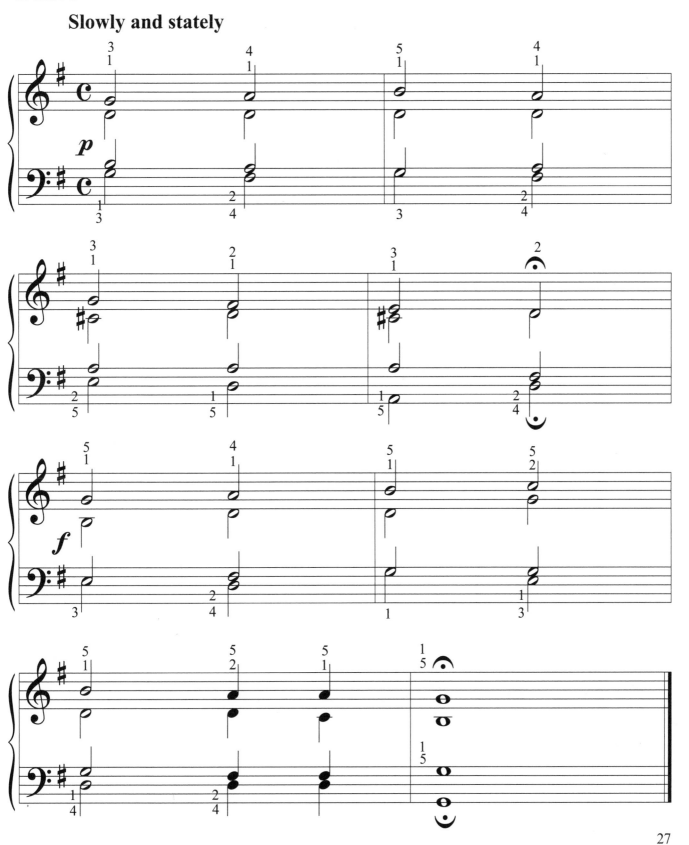

First Loss

Schumann was from a period in music known as the Romantic Era. It was more emotional than the previous, called Classical, which focused on neatness and restraint. Be expressive, and use the dynamics to help.

Slowly and sweetly

Little Etude

Etudes are musical pieces focusing on a particular exercise. Here, both hands are being stretched and learning to work together. Always be even with your tempo and keep your eyes looking forward.

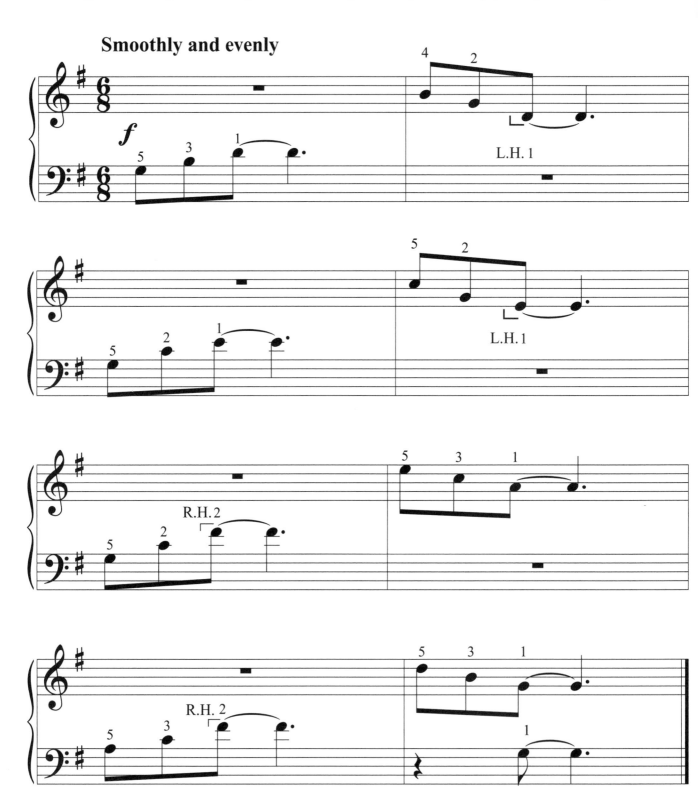

Happy Farmer

Schumann would often escape to the country to relax, and this work describes one of his many joyful trips. You may have heard the melody before: it was played in *The Wizard of Oz*.

Moderato

Reaper's Song

Schumann recreates a rustic atmosphere by using wide intervals in the left hand. These octaves and fifths are known as "open harmonies" and mimic early country instruments. When playing, paint the scene using these old sounds.

Andante

Morning Roaming

Triplets are three even notes in one beat, marked with a slanted 3. Don't be tempted to rush. Rather, think of them as fractions with each being ⅓ of a quarter note—just like each eighth note is ½ of a quarter note.

Andante

Wild Rider

This exciting melody is built on arpeggios. Warm-up with A minor and E major arpeggios and you'll find the right hand easier to play. Use the left hand to accent the "gallop."

At a gallop

34

Symphonic Etudes
(theme)

Schumann composed 12 very complex and colorful variations around this simple theme. They were so broad and big sounding that they were named "symphonic." Use the chromatic scale in measure 2 to add color to the melody.

Stately, and not too fast

Scherzo
from Symphony No. 4

Schumann wrote four symphonies in all. This *scherzo* is from the third movement of Symphony No. 4. Notice how the melody is echoed—bounce the music back and forth between the hands.

Allegro moderato

Piano Quintet

(opening)

A piano quintet is an ensemble consisting of a piano, 2 violins, viola, and cello. This piece was premiered by Clara Schumann at the piano and a circle of friends on strings. Don't rush, and project a majestic sound.

Allegro moderato

Piano Concerto
(opening)

Schumann was a very promising young pianist. Unfortunately, he permanently injured his right hand and couldn't perform. Although he wrote many short piano pieces, he wrote only one concerto.

Allegro

Pappillons

Schumann lived during the development of "Program Music"—a style of composing meant to represent objects and people. Pappillon means "butterfly," and the work is filled with images representing flight. There are even two sections for one hand only.

Intro

II. Left Hand Only

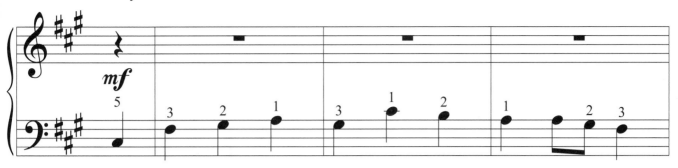

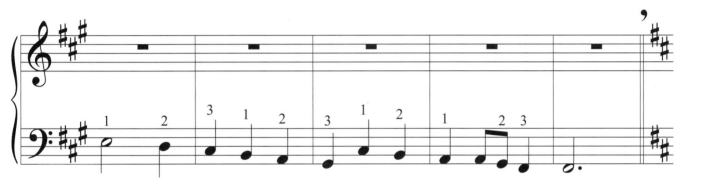

III. Right Hand Only

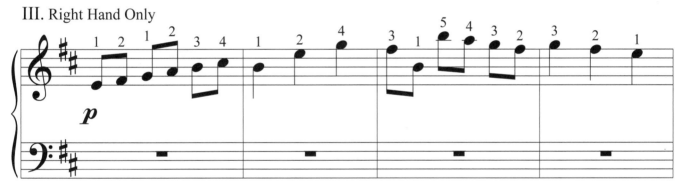

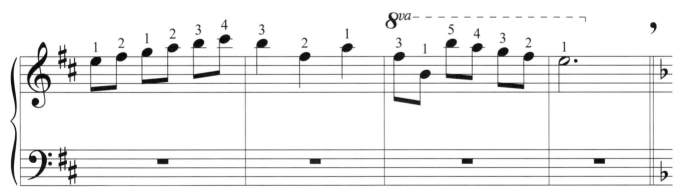

IV.

V. Finale